First published in North America
by Annick Press, 2006
Text © 2005 Meg Clibbon
Illustrations © 2005 Lucy Clibbon
Originally published by Zero to Ten Limited
(a member of the Evans Publishing Group)
© 2005 Zero to Ten Limited

Cataloging in Publication
Clibbon, Meg
Imagine you're a ballerina! / Margot Fountainpen, Lucy Leotard.
(Imagine this! series)
ISBN-13: 978-1-55451-020-7 (bound)
ISBN-10: 1-55451-020-1 (bound)
ISBN-13: 978-1-55451-019-1 (pbk.)
ISBN-10: 1-55451-019-8 (pbk.)
1. Ballerinas--Juvenile literature.   2. Ballet--Juvenile literature.
I. Clibbon, Lucy II. Title. III. Series: Clibbon, Meg. Imagine this! series.

GV1787.5.C52 2006   j792.802'8092   C2006-901212-1

www.annickpress.com

Printed in China

Imagine you're a
Ballerina!

Lucy Leotard

trained at the Twinkletoes Academy of Dance. She was a prima ballerina for a glorious but brief period before suffering an unfortunate accident while being swept off her feet by a leading man. This enforced an early retirement and a career change to art and design. She now creates costumes, posters, and stage sets for the ballet world.

Margot Fountainpen

learned ballet from an early age, and starred as a sunflower when she was five. Now all her petals have fallen off so she writes about ballet instead.

To Assis Carreiro and DanceEast

Annick Press Ltd.

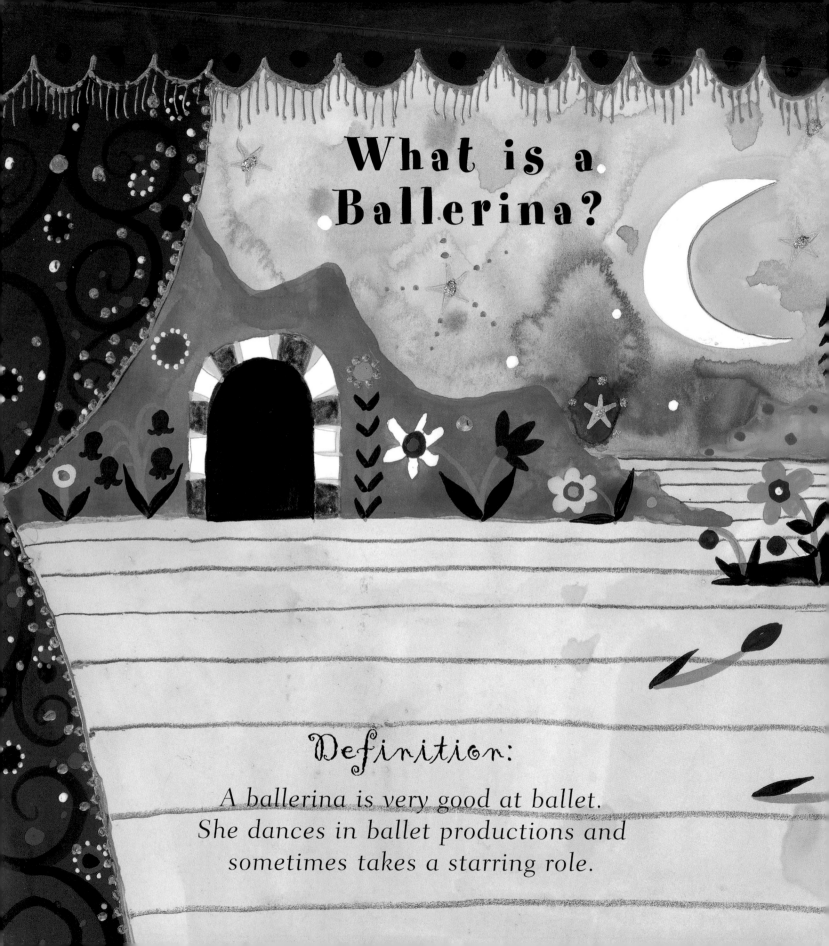

What is a Ballerina?

Definition:

A ballerina is very good at ballet.
She dances in ballet productions and
sometimes takes a starring role.

The History of Ballet

The word ballet means "a dance." Ballet started long ago when kings and queens and their courtiers loved to dance with set steps and movements. These dances were graceful and rather theatrical with beautiful costumes, mimes, and music. Gradually, with the formation of the first ballet academies, some of the steps and movements were written down and passed on to the next generation of dancers.

As ballets became more popular, they were shown in theaters too, although women were forbidden to appear onstage.

In 1681 at the Paris Opéra, women were at last allowed to dance onstage. This was really the start of ballet dancing as we know it. The footwork and flowing movements became more intricate.

One or two ballet dancers tried dancing on tiptoe. This new technique was very popular and led to many of the steps used by choreographers today.

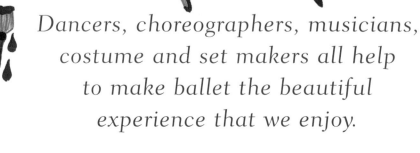

Dancers, choreographers, musicians, costume and set makers all help to make ballet the beautiful experience that we enjoy.

Becoming a Ballerina

Everyone can have fun dancing. Anyone can have ballet lessons, but only a few special people become ballerinas. To be a real ballerina you need to have the right kind of body and train that body to work very hard.

You must love music and learn how to fit ballet movements to music. You have to be very dedicated to be a ballerina and you do it for the joy of performing beautiful dances for other people to appreciate.

Ballet School

There are several very famous ballet schools where the pupils are taught to be good at dancing as well as learning all the other subjects. Auditions are held where you have to show how flexible you are. If you show the right potential you may be accepted to join a very special group of students and one day you may become a ballerina.

# In the Studio

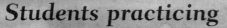
Students practicing

Costumes hanging up

Bar

Tutu stands

Piano

Pointe shoes

Ballet teacher

Ballerinas need a lot of practice. This always starts at the bar. You hold the bar at the side of the room and do a series of exercises starting with the plié, which means "bend." Ballerinas are very bendy.

Choreography

Choreography is a long word but it means the art of putting particular steps to music. It is very important because, if dancers just dance any old steps, they might crash into each other and this would ruin the ballet. Choreographers are essential to the art of ballet. Famous choreographers include Martha Graham, Jerome Robbins, and George Balanchine.

Basic positions

 First

 Second

These are elementary positions learned by all ballet students.

Third

Fifth

 Fourth

Ballet Language

A French king started the first ballet school, in 1661, so now the language of ballet is French. Here are some French ballet terms:

Pirouette
spinning around and around without falling over

Arabesque
holding a beautiful shape on one leg without falling over

Pas de deux
dancing with a partner without knocking him over

Corps de ballet
a group of dancers who perform together
without knocking each other over

Ballet words

Can you see which letters are missing from this list?

B_r
Orchest_a
B_llet
_allerina
L_otard
_tudio
_uick!
T_tu
Flow_rs

Ballerina Do's and Don'ts

What ballerinas must do:

1. Learn to point their toes

2. Eat healthily

3. Learn French

4. Respect the dance teacher

What ballerinas must not do:

1. Miss dance classes

2. Wear the wrong shoes

3. Break a leg

4. Get angry with their partners (who might drop them)

Equipment and Accessories

Tutus – fancy little dresses

Hairnet – keeps hair tidy

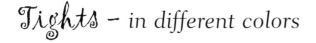

Tights – in different colors

Ballet shoes – lots of pairs

Makeup

Hair spray

Leg Warmers

Wigs

What Do Ballerinas Wear?

Each ballet has special costumes worn by ballerinas.

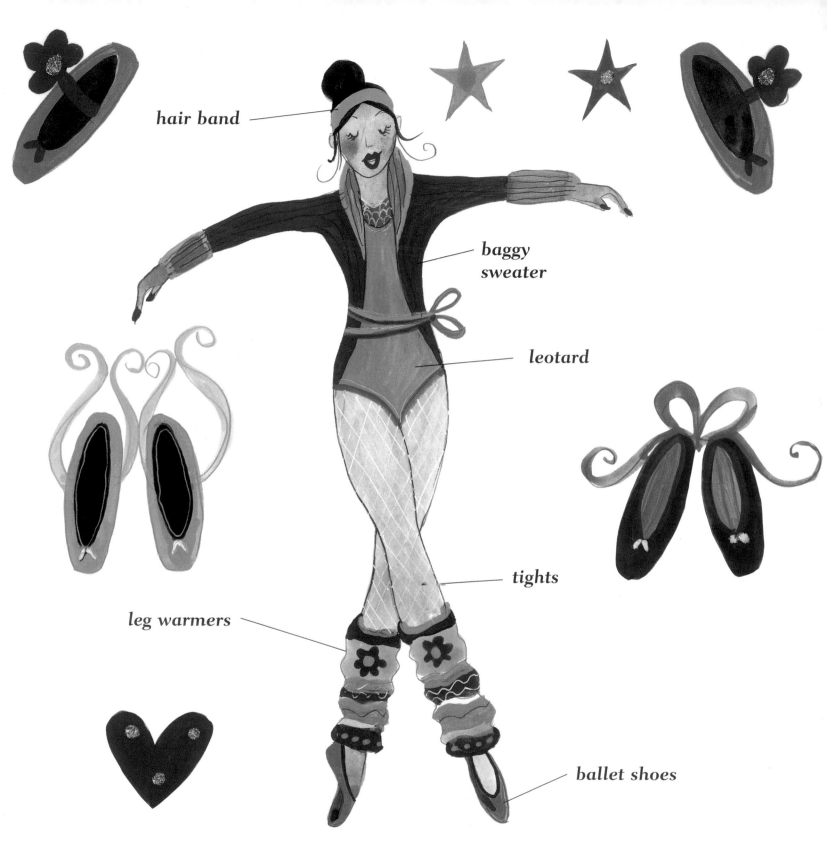

hair band

baggy sweater

leotard

tights

leg warmers

ballet shoes

However, during practice a ballerina looks more like this.

Famous Ballets

Classical ballets are very popular, and the amazing thing is that very strange stories are made to become realistic and beautiful when danced by ballet dancers.

Giselle is about the spirit of a young girl that dances around a graveyard at midnight with lots of other spirits.

Swan Lake is about how a prince falls in love with a swan and after falling in a lake they live happily ever after.

The Nutcracker involves fighting mice, a mysterious clockmaker, and snowflakes.

Coppelia is about how a girl, Swanilda, pretends to be a clockwork doll in order to make her boyfriend love her.

Rite of Spring is about pagans leaping around the stage and enjoying misbehaving themselves until one dies.

Romeo and Juliet is about how Romeo loves Juliet and Juliet loves Romeo. They die beautifully.

Interview with a Ballerina

Madame Nellie Topolova is interviewed
by Lily Legwarmer for "Ballet Zone."

Lily: Madame Topolova, when did you begin in ballet?

Madame Nellie: I first danced
when I am a little, little
girl. I dance and dance
until my feet bleed, but
still I keep dancing
because I love it so.

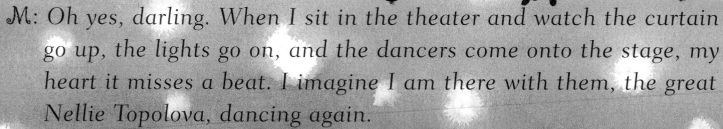

L: Do you still love it?

M: Oh yes, darling. When I sit in the theater and watch the curtain
go up, the lights go on, and the dancers come onto the stage, my
heart it misses a beat. I imagine I am there with them, the great
Nellie Topolova, dancing again.

𝓛: Now that you no longer perform, you run a school for young dancers, don't you?

𝓜: The little darlings! How they love me! They learn so much. I make them work, but still they love me.

𝓛: What was your greatest moment?

𝓜: When I dance for the Royal Family with the great Sergei Slipoff.

𝓛: What was your worst moment?

𝓜: When he drop me!

𝓛: Thank you so much, Madame. You are an inspiration to us all.

At the theater

Royal box

Cheering

Clapping

Flowers

Famous ballerinas

There have been many very famous ballerinas including
Anna Pavlova (who had a pudding named after her),
Dame Margot Fonteyn, and Karen Kain.
One day perhaps your name will become just as famous.

Boys and ballet

Boys at ballet school are taught to be very strong. Male dancers have to
support and hold up their partners. They have to leap very high in the
air and perform very strenuous routines. They combine strength and
flexibility with grace and drama. Ballerinas cannot do their work
without good partners. Some famous male dancers include
Rudolf Nureyev, Mikhail Baryshnikov, and Rex Harrington.

Things to do

Dolly tutus

Cut a long piece of net, which is as wide as your doll's leg measured from waist to knee. Thread a needle and sew along one long edge.

Pull the thread into gathers and tie the tutu around the doll's waist.

Ballet scrapbook

Collect anything you can find to do with ballet – swans' feathers, photographs of famous dancers, advertisements for ballet performances, programs, and scraps of material from costumes. Stick them into the scrapbook and decorate each page beautifully.

Pavlovas

Fill ready-made meringue shells with whipped cream and strawberries. Trickle berry juice over each one. Fluffy as a tutu – but filling!